Burned
A journey in mental health literature
written by **Louis Irvine**

This is my story from my perspective
dealing with mental health problems.
You will read through
many different experiences.
From dark times to brighter days.
It's pretty much a lifestyle.
If you are reading this
all you need to do is program the mind
to never forget that phases come and go.
Your strength will determine the
outcome.

I truly wish you all the best in life.
~
I hope you find comfort in this book.

It seeped through, leaving me completely confused.
A spectator of my own self yet again.
Suffering through those dark nights trapped in the most brainstorming of all cataclysmic journeys,
unwillingly created within the psyche.
Endurance, exhaustion.
Remind thyself it will be over soon.

Close your eyes, everything will be fine
"It can't be... still"?
"Stop"!
"Don't let it begin".
Your world has been still for a while now.
Minutes and hours turn into lost days.
Nothing exists.
There is no meaning
or purpose to anything.
Confusion.
Curtains closed with eyes of
nothingness.
Trying to take back what is truly yours,
or is it?
Seperating realities reminding yourself
that this is the universe challenging you.
But for what?
The journey will end soon.

Seated at the corner of the bed I hold it in.
No one must see the suffering.
It gets a little intense at the top of the bed where the head should rest.
Shutter speed visuals of destruction throughout my existence penetrate my core leaving no choice but to back down and open my eyes, for now.
The corner of the bed holds alot of ache.
Moments of madness
to uncontrollable crying and trembling as my wife holds me like a newborn.
I tried...
I tried to hold it in.

Soft breaths turn to an outweighed gasp
for one last time as you try to steer the
mind toward a cause.
Chaos reigns down trying to zone in.
The motherboard fully activated sends
waves of overwhelming tingles
throughout the body.
You forget about that last breath
as you are helplessly dragged through
sheer carnage of the
central nervous system.
Suddenly, released,
the mind focuses on that last breath.
Intermission?
Confusion and overthinking settle in
leaving only fear of what's coming
when I close my eyes.
Breathe.

Hunched shoulders, clutched tightly,
wrapped in a cocoon of my own sweat.
The nights are long.
Days don't exist.
The lungs fill up
breaking the deafening silence,
as a moment before all that existed
was the feeling of a
single droplet flowing downward
onto the mattress beneath.
You were that droplet.
It existed therefore you exist,
but nothing else did.
Finger tip imprints fade from my
shoulders as I let go.

"There isn't enough time".
Heard with confusion
through trembling lips.
I know not why or what for,
but all I know is there isn't enough time.
Am I connected to something much
bigger that perhaps only a few have
reached?
Why is there not enough time?
There's meaning for everything
yet no meaning for this.
Or is there?
Neuronic shutters from
overly apprehensive behaviour
zap like a cattle prod.
A torturous reminder
that this vessel is still on auto-pilot.
Am I delving too deep, too fast?
I have no control.
Is this all a challenge to see how far
you can reach inside your own mind?
Time will tell.

Will I ever get a break?
The thought of not wanting to be here hovers once again as my stomach unbearably churns.
I glimpse at my wife as she stares on distracted over my fidgeting silence.
I wish she had a better life away from me.
I just want it to end.
Heat radiates throughout my body as my chest begins to tighten.
Eyes dry with exhaustion.
Relentless yawns yet not a wink slept.
The hope of escape from this world to a never-ending dream state faded.
Understanding?
Someday.

I can't do this for much longer.
Thoughts of suicide circulate,
weighing me down.
I hear my wife humming a lullaby to our
youngest in the next room.
I love them so much.
Their lives are wasted with me around.
Time heals.
They can still have fun stress free lives.
My inner malfunctions are worn out.
This can't go on for forever,
can it?
Everything is calm now.
Who am I?

Black, black, black...
Repeatedly echoes trying to throw thoughts off guard in a hope of sneaking into utopia.
Everything is calm, but something appears.
It's a face staring at me
with a vile smirk and darkness in its eyes.
It does not mean well.
Immediately backing down,
I open my eyes.
"You won't win tonight predatory thought".
Welcome insomnia.
Four nights pass, not a wink slept.
Convincing myself that I am evolving into something of superior power.
The Illusoury Truth Effect.
I wake up in a hospital bed, overdosed.

I don't want to be here
yet, I never want to leave.
Need more ups than downs,
more ups than downs
(echoes through my mind)
Life shouldn't hurt.
No one should have to suffer.
It's all a game that I'd rather not play.
Voices lost in the night.
We are all one, yet seperated.
Deep concious awareness
needs to light up the world.
Like a flame in the darkest cave.
We are off track.
This world isn't for me.

Extortion of the mind.
Moving forward on a positive vibe,
kind of a rare occasion.
We all deserve it.
The nervous system sends out pulses.
Only in times like these they are
euphoric.
With every pulse triggering butterflies
in your throat.
You are ontop of the highest mountain
visualizing letting the joy within
echo as far as it can reach.
Feeling that deep breath
make you whole again.
I understand why there isn't enough time.
These occasions remind you that there is
still part of you in there.
Never forget that.
Carrying strength many won't experience
for moments like these makes
living that more worth while.
Train the mind to never lose yourself.

Perimeter breach.
Brain fog and tilted vision
in social gatherings.
Breaking that confidence
you felt moments before.
Now creating more unsettling thought
patterns as to what the reason is behind
these disorders, or is it all linked?
Am I just one big destructive mess that
has no chance at a life?
If I shake my head hard enough
will it disrupt the cycle?
Scrambling for cover the earthquake
within gives time for a breath
and empty thought.
Perimeter secure, for now.

Paths are long.
Lungs are tight.
Observing as far as the eye can see.
Analytic thought patterns begin.
Assuming the outside world
are all clear minded as I dig myself deeper
imagining family and friends contacting one another to say I finally gave in.
I don't know where these thoughts will take me but I will fight this to my last breath. Never submitting to the darkness within.
I hope one day peace will consume me.
I wonder if people get sick of happiness.
If only I could live my fullest life.
The things I believe I could accomplish.
I could be a prophet.
Can darkness be that powerful shielding such fortune?

Sadness, fear, anger.
Joy, passion, relief.
Heart rate up and down.
Exhausted, lonely, agonised.
Meditative, determined, optimistic.
Do you feel embarrassed,
confused or scared?
You are not alone.
Embrace every emotion.
Ignorance is bliss.
Mould yourself.
Your experiences should not be wasted.
Spark the flame around you.
Shine through the darkness.
Your life has purpose.

Love.
What does it mean
when you have a mental illness?
How can one focus on love when they are so absorbed by their own thoughts, leaving no time to let it bunk the queue.
You understand love in a way that supersedes what most describe as feeling such an emotion, yet through the cycle
it gets lost entering those involved into a lonely uncomfortable thought process of confusion, yet somewhat understanding.
There's unfairness for both parties.
It makes focusing soley on surviving another day tiring
with understandable extra baggage.
We all strive for the freedom to feel love and rightly so, it keeps us moving forward.
Find your way to express it again.
Love is the key to everything.

Everyday is the same.
Life is frozen.
We are a single blip in the
existence of the universe.
Yet so many of us suffer so much pain.
What's worse for many is that
it's not even at our own hands or through
our own choices.
What we are exposed to as kids
moulds us into what we are today.
Leading us down two paths,
pleasant or nasty.
Consequences are inevitable,
regardless of the direction.
The older you get
the more it can make or break you.
The ache will never go away, but you
can learn to manage and understand
yourself.
Reach these levels and
you will become enlightened,
viewing the world unlike the masses.

Do this first, have fun later.
The mind isn't just a voice.
Stuck in a time warp,
losing grip of reality.
Don't follow the herd.
How do you cope with the pain and fear?
It's hard not to lose yourself
with the endless pressure.
Emotions run deep.
Imprinted from a child.
Theres no escape, nowhere to hide.
So you switched to drugs, just for a while.
It isn't a cure,
but damn it feels good to be high.
You are responsible for few.
Never let them in.
They'll only succumb to what's within,
tearing them apart, never let them in.
Break the habit.

Negative thoughts run deep,
Wish they would end so I can sleep.
Pitch black, tossin and turnin,
stomach churnin,
medication beyond working.
Every night is the same.
This isn't a game.
It's exhausting just breathing.
So I turn to my pad and write down these
thoughts as the mind is dragged
like a carcass down a hole.
Wondering where I'm being lead and
what the outcome will be.
Just another night, a passenger in flight.
Bare foot, haven't earned shoes yet.
Time to step up.
Tables have turned, bridges burned.
Disconnecting from this world is hard to
do,
but I need too.
Worlds within a world.

I saw a video online where someone was asked about their father.
He said his dad abandoned him and his mother when he was a child and that he had died.
He answers the questions with a smile and laughter.
Upon reading the comments I came across one where someone said that his laughing and smiling were hiding his tears.
I replied,
"no they're not".

Imprisoned for 7 years when I was 2
The man who impregnated my mother was once my dad, but no longer holds that title and hasn't done for roughly 28 years
He abandoned my mother and I with my new born baby brother.
I was 11.
What we aren't going to do is ever mention him again.

I never had a permanent home until now.
A wife and three kids, I feel secure now.
As a child life was full of ups and downs.
The older I got, it seemed like more downs, downs, downs.
I accepted it though, because it was real.
I had to adapt and grow.
Younger than most.
All the while keeping it hidden like a ghost.
Home to home, hostel to hostel.
It became natural.
I could always see the struggle and pain in her eyes, but at the same time,
she drank burying it deep inside.
I hated her, I loved her, it was hell for years.
No wonder it's passed on drowning me in tears.
I'm exhausted and done.
One thing,
this will never happen to my sons.

I had the best of everything.
I got anything I wanted, but now I see that was pay off for invisible guilt.
She will never be the blame.
If only you could fathom this.
All we want is to feel secure and loved.
Face your problems early on before they stack up leaving more darkness than light.
Theres no shame in struggle or being open.
Everyone has problems.
It's how you cope with them that makes you fully understand who you are.
So, keep it tight.

I have three children now.
This is all for them.
I'll fight the darkness
until there's nothing left.
Hope was gone.
We were helpless and lost.
What would you do in this train of thought?
We are who we are.
There's a reason for it all.
I have no regrets.
I'm pleased I've come this far.
Demanding the understanding of what operates within and why its functions have put a grin on my face the older I get.
I'm not gonna lie, times were hard to the point of only seeing death.
Phases come and go, let it be known.
At the end of the day life fades away.
Choose your path and pray.

Things take time.
Clean it out.
I don't feel guilty for what I believe or want.
Level me up!
I believe I've felt and seen everything one should and I'm only 36.
We can't predict our future;
but judging by how it's panned out so far, the exhaustion involved for another 30 years isn't a great sales pitch.
These are just thoughts though.
I'm stronger than most and on a level of lyrical thinking that surpasses many.
I used to think I was weird, when I began wondering who I was.
It had me paranoid beyond anyones knowledge.
The herd is for the weak.
None are stronger than those who can be alone.

Learn to be alone.
Legacy is for ego driven narcissists.
It doesn't matter to me,
if I don't matter when I'm gone.
This world makes no sense to the deep thinkers because we want a different world, a world where we can all feel full and explore together as one race, the human race.
There's nothing wrong with ambition, but in a world so corrupt there is no purpose to some.
They know the game is rigged, leaving them to wonder; what's the point sacrificing energy?
A small percentage of the planet is run by the wrong kind.
Everything needs to change.
Knowing what many of us know is exhausting because it won't end well for the masses.

Farewell.
Choose your final track as you transition to the next level of consciousness.
What would yours be?
Humanity isn't the be all and end all of existence.
I don't believe in heaven and hell.
I believe we are one consciousness experiencing seperate realities, but are all connected as one infinite energy source.
Who you see in the mirror is just a vessel.
The energy within you will still be here after the transition.
I can't help but wonder; will we roam free throughout the universe, truly embracing what we should be working toward experiencing on a human level?

We are here.
There has to be more.
Weeks have passed.
Breathing and smiling feels good.
Bursts of tranquility are so euphoric and a reminder that all experiences are a gift, good or bad.
Finding the right music to enhance these bursts can be an incredible boost for getting the most out of peaceful occasions.
The ache is always there.
Knowing these moments are a crucial point in the mind of one who suffers.
So breathe and smile uncontrollably.
Remember you are on your own unique journey that no one has to understand, but you.
Use these positive moments to train the mind towards a new way of operating.
Your mind is an endless mechanism.

Drug abuse.
I knew she knew.
She knew, I knew that she knew,
but we always played it dumb.
It takes the pain away so much making you disappear, but you are also distancing yourself from your family at the same time.
It releases you from that uncontrollable agony that circulates the mind and body.
Temporary fix for everlasting torture.
From finding yourself somewhat focused on life, to everything being flipped upside down and you're life now focused on getting that rush of euphoric bliss.
You get lost so easily.
You just want to be alone regretting everything your life has led up to.
You know you have responsibilities, but you'd rather not face them because there is already too much to deal with.

Locking yourself away in a dark room feels like freedom.
It can't be that easy forever.
The world is overrun with addicts in horrible conditions so why would it not end that way for me or you?
It will.
If you built up the courage to turn your back on everything that holds the structure intact you will meet your inevitable demise.
When you accept you're addicted, then and only then try moving forward.
That's if you're willing too.

You are invincible during manic episodes.
You feel like you can walk through a brick wall.

Engaging in risky behaviours,
juggling an addictive personality.
Knowing you suffer from this disorder,
yet, continuing down the road of
whatever you're fixation is at the time
despite the negative consequences.
Swinging from prescription and
stimulant drugs to gambling,
over eating and loss of appetite.
Chemical and behavioural addiction both
linger bouncing from one to the other
as quick as snapping your fingers.
I guess it's all part of a
mental health disorders structure.
There is always time to seek help, but
the process in this day and age
is like a warzone.
Going from psychologist to psychologist
feels like a game of pass the parcel with
each giving their own perspective leaving
you overwhelmed and somewhat even

more lost not knowing what's what
or who's calling next.
Cravings come out of nowhere leading to selfish ways, but you're subconciously just trying to escape underlying conditions.
We didn't grow up saying to ourselves this is what we want to be.
Guess it is what it is.
No point blaming those who subjected you to severe trauma.
If seeking help is this difficult nowadays with suicide rates through the roof; then the older generation had no hope.
As you get older, you understand in their situation help was much more scarce; considering awareness and technology wasn't as advanced.
You can't choose the life
you were born into.

"If I cant get you when you're awake,
I'll get you in your dreams".
My mind feeling liberation only to be given a reminder when my eyes close, let the games begin!
Waking up crying and screaming then wanting to get back into the dream to defeat the invisible enemy.
Sometimes, if you are lucky you can enter the same dream at the exit point.
I used to look forward to going to bed saying to my wife
"I can't wait to see where I end up tonight."
Sometimes dreams can feel better than the real world.
If only we could record our dreams and watch them over.
The chaos, destruction, delight, joy, whatever may lurk
would be interesting to see.

Maybe that's one of the beautiful gifts we are treated to as humans.
Experiencing a dreamstate where present and locked away thoughts can be moulded together creating absolute madness, but out of it all is a reminder that
even when asleep the subconscious is always at work.
When you look at a picture of the universe imagine that is your dreamstate and
you can end up anywhere.
It's beautifully mindblowing to think about.
Something beautiful is waiting for all of us.
I believe it.
You should too.
I don't want a heaven.
I want to travel through space and time for eternity.
The universe holds billions of galaxies,

we should be entitled to visit them all.

Lately I've been alone.
Seperating myself
from all kinds of negativity.
Kind of stuff I'll take to my grave.
Feels good to be free now.
No worries for a while now.
Blocked off certain roads.
Going solo now.
Bumps in the road, got to steer clear.
Can't carry the weight on my shoulders
and attend to myself at the same time.
It's me, myself and I.
I'm not selfish.
It kills me at times, but it has to be done.
We have to find our own paths
before we get lost.
Only fake people get annoyed
when you speak realness.
PTSD forever.
I can live with the scars.
I know who I am.

Tears dried up recently.
Dark emotions are numb.
Slowly feeling the "norm" of normality.
Thoughts are overwhelming.
Got that lump in my throat.
Pride.
Feels strange.
My body isn't used to the calmness.
Feel bored.
Sleeping alot better now.
Damaged dreams trouble me though.
Days look brighter.
Head held high, feeling unstoppable.
Gotta stay focused.
What goes up must come down.
Let's not worry about that now.
Embrace the joy like you embrace the dark.
Never look back.
It ain't over yet.

The realisation that issues
will come and go is inevitable.
All we can do is help one another if
we feel strong enough to seek it.
Like myself though, many will find
comfort
in their own quiet place.
Whilst siblings worry that this isn't the
answer, we ourselves understand in our
own minds that all we want is
peace in those moments.
There will be times when you feel the
urge to seek professional help, but in
today's world getting that help looks to
be like a
full-time job.
Never give up on yourself.
I say it time and time again,
embrace every single emotion.
This is what makes you human,
and in my opinion the purest of all.

Work life can be a serious struggle.
Especially when old peers intimidated you.
Many can relate.
An unexpected, uneducated moment on ones behalf, gave me an ultimatum; sort your mental health out within a week, or do not return, unpaid, until you do.
To this day it has never sat right with me.
These perpetrators don't realise that those who seriously struggle, leave such interactions replaying the situation over and over again in their mind to the point of a mental breakdown.
Whilst they aren't at all phased and go on with their daily life like it was nothing.
It's your job to try and make your life easier for your own sanity.
Never ever back down.
The ignorance will never be forgotten.

They've no idea what they're dealing with.
They need more guidance than you.

If life ever grants you the opportunity to interact with someone unknowingly repetitive in your social life, enlighten yourself by absorbing that experience, breaking the psyche that you have consciously known.
Realise that we are all unique.
Never to elaborate our usual mindset, expressions outside our culture,
but to embrace the moment and know that we know we have reached levels of embracing the world as endless.

I goes
She goes
He goes
We goes
They goes
One by one maintaining false lives.
Hoping, if educated enough on the topic,
understand and accept what drags one
through the mud; that experiencing a
breakthrough could possibly lessen the
burden of dealing with the extreme mind
one has been inflicted with.
The mask rarely comes off.
Reaching the point of no return
where too many have sadly fallen.
Surrendering to the misery
is in itself a breaking point.
That negative outcome could be your
chance to breakthrough that
breaking point, to embrace to your core
what you are experiencing.

Levels of darkness that only
the chosen can speak upon.
It doesn't have to be seen as a problem,
but as a seismic challenge that
you can try mastering.
Giving you the opportunity to one day
open up to the world and possibly
reach out to many who are
secretly suffering.
It could be your destiny.
Angels of Earth, forever flawed,
accepting their path in life.
You are you for a reason.
Be you and only you.
No one can be anyone but themselves,
so accept who you are
and see where it takes you.
This journey could be just the beginning.
No one truly knows what's to come.
How goes it?

A dream within a dream.
Whilst dreaming your dream,
within that dream is a concious state.
You know it's a dream
and are able to watch the role play out,
but for me, like a normal dream
you have no control over what happens.
My experiences usually take effect when
I'm in a reoccurring dream.
Sometimes picking up from where
it left off and other times
from different perspectives.
The dream within a dream is always
anxiety fueled like the majority of
my main dreamstates.
A fascinating experience,
but hard to put into words.

I felt this strange energy last night.
I can't describe it.
It was so unsettling I had to set up camp
in my living room and put my head down.
I slowly made my way back up to bed
as the hours past.
I eventually fell asleep.
Ready for work the next morning,
off I went.
Shortly after I received a voice note.
Her voice was trembling.
Overwhelming screaming heard
in the background as I got word that
another friend had surrendered
to his unknown suffering.
I wish I had of known.
He knew about my experiences, but
bravely held onto his own torment.
We need serious guidance.
Smiles no more.

Horrific deafening screams.
Devastation.
Trauma yet again.
There's no manual to life.
We will never know what's around the corner.
Opening up to the world about serious issues daily, hoping that even the people living closest to you will find a format to cope.
When you witness a tragic event that overtakes and smothers someone to the point of no return; it's extremely damaging to see loved ones out of their minds with what is probably the most grievous experience they'll ever go through. Empathising, looking from their point of view, where they are mentally is unsettling because you fight for survival everyday.

At the moment of writing this, im acutely aware that speaking out in an attempt to bring awareness to those who are secretly suffering may still be futile.
Some will still end it all, because the mind is a dangerous place that should be feared for what it can create.
You gave it your all and it will never be looked upon as selfish or weak.
You held on for as long as you could.
That is bravery.
Those who believe it is selfish to leave loved ones behind have never experienced, or witnessed someone go through the personal horrors they suffer and must deal with.
If they did, they would realise that the torment was too overwhelming
to put up with and the need to escape it.
Well,
there is only one outcome for the majority.

It's extremely devastating, but remember everyone is left in their own mind 24/7 and no matter how much you try to be there to console them. It won't be enough.
The mind is serious business.
It's extremely hard to switch off when it takes a turn for the worst.
I myself have been a veteran of suffering and although I've overdosed and self harmed, I've managed to make myself aware to always remember that it will pass.
It's just a vicious circle of ups and downs.
You will forever be remembered.
Your energy is now free from this disease.
If we can make it known and embedded into the psyche that it's nothing to be embarrassed about, then maybe we can move in a positive direction
saving as many lives as possible.

Life is a game.
Many of us come with disadvantages
unable to operate to the
highest of our ability.
A mental illness can beat you
into the ground then vanish.
In these moments you can breathe again
with endless ideas for success.
This is when there isn't enough time.
You are never given
the opportunity to even begin,
but remember,
in the time you have, it can be seen as
an unfinished project that can one day
be carried on again as if you never even
departed in the first place.

The world is changing.
What you once knew will be no more.
Chaos is everywhere
at an uncontrollable rate.
Try not to get sucked in.
It will become more and more noticeable
as we progress through the coming
years.
Your mind is the true you.
Don't keep it locked away.
Stand tall and proud.
Never surrender to anothers influence.
Conciously and subconciously stay
aware.
Never lose sight.
No one can experience being you.
Let the real you be free of fear.
No one cares.
We are all on our own journeys.
Some more than others.
A mindset is the path to
whatever you desire.

Try not to worry.
The pressure will fade someday.
Jeopardy is familiar.
Your wounds are distant memories.
Don't be afraid.
Your shoulders carry tremendous weight.
You are still here.
Don't give up.
Hold on.
Smile.
Change is hard.
Lives are strange.
Make your world important.
Escape the infestation.
You've been there for far too long.

Reality
Infinite substances
The natural sciences
Layers of the universe
Objective
Subjective
Injustice
Known
Unknown
Being
Thinking
Knowledge
Each of us percieve the world through our own eyes which means reality varies from person to person,
but it never changes.
Reality is what it is.
Reality is fact.

You see.
She knows.
Comforting acceptance.
Emotions wrapped up.
Looking for a side glance.
Motions of a slow dance in the romance,
last forever.
The warmth of your whisper echoes.
Eyes locked.
Losing control in the darkness.
Head rush has me falling for you.
Take my hand as we runaway.
You try to kiss me.
My heart has never felt like this.
Tender actions passionately exploding.
We explore with a gentle touch.
Our eyes close.
Energy unmatched.

Left with dreams.
There's no place to run.
I can't leave.
Looking back.
Waiting all my life.
I want to look until I see the void.
Stargazing as shadows pass.
Strangers to themselves.
Do you want to feel how it feels?
Ripping and tearing.
If I tell you will you remain calm?
Then you will see what I really see.
It hurts.
Can you feel this?
Forever free falling.
Would you catch me?

Caught in the moment.
We move in circles.
Don't cry.
It's not over.
Inbetween the spaces.
Look for me.
I will guide you.
The voices burn within.
Follow my footprints.
Don't fall off the path.
Searching for answers.
The time is almost here.
Don't forget about me.
We get a moment.
Frozen.
Our vibrations connected.
Deep rhythmic movements.
A state of mind.

I need to kill myself to get my point across

I've been out of place for quite some time.
Its been so rough.
I've tried to explain, but
it doesn't come out how I want it too.
You can witness with your eyes
the moments I can't see your face.
The darkness leaves me locked away.
The world closed off, for their own sake.
But I know I've got you.
At least I know, when it's time,
I can confide in you.
I hope it never gets too much for you.
You mystify me.
It brings me peace to know you care.
It gives me hope because you are there.
You make life seem so fair.
Making me feel whole again.
I take a breath and bow my head.

Gravity pulls us down whilst bubbles rise.
Grip onto me.
Never let go.
We will sink together.
You have watched my destruction
for quite some time.
Most wouldn't stick around.
You did.
You're perfect in every way.
Can you remember when we first met?
Can you remember how it felt?
Here we are over 20 years later.
It seems like forever.
You're the only one I care about.
All we need are one another.

Spread your wings and carry me.
Where will we end up?
Mental health isn't a destination.
I turn my head to see your face.
Cloud surfing.
We chase the wind.
We have covered so much ground.
You wipe my scars with the softest touch.
Tears melt away the pain.
I reach out and touch you.
Showing you an invisible world.
Darkness turns to light.
We reflect each other.

Dark skies.
Misty rain swirls.
Gently hides your tears.
Endless walks along the stormy sea.
A wave of depression.
Crushing the chest.
Squelching on sand dunes.
Knee deep,
your fingertips caress the water.
In the distance a beacon radiates warmth.
One deep breath.
You are immersed.
Slowly sinking.
Foggy eyes staring up.
Light breaks through.
Bubbles glisten.
Surfacing.
Feeling the rays on your skin.
Reborn.

Innocent eyes broken.
They begin to fill up.
They glisten from the light above.
Attempting to control it,
your vibrations are beginning to break.
That indescribable feeling leaks through.
Everyone can see you're invisible pain.
You shield yourself with your backpack.
Gripping onto it tightly.
You seen their lips moving,
but couldn't hear anything they said.
Eye contact tells alot if you feel what I feel.

The mirror never laughs at me.
It shows my tears but it's okay,
because it never laughs at me.
So many times I've tried to hurt myself.
I've overdosed and self harmed
during a manic episodes.
I came close to leaving my vessel.
I'm still here and you're still here with me.
You've seen the darkness within me.
Still, you never left my side.
Steering me toward never forgetting
who I should be.
You are now a piece of the puzzle.
Without you it would never be complete.
You're my deepest friend.

The wandering mind
has a mind of its own.
Attempting to depict a tragic outcome
where I climb into my bath
slitting my wrists behind my back
so it doesn't spray everywhere
leaving a mess.
The conversation continues,
debating whether there would be
enough time to do so, so whoever finds me
won't have to clean up the mess.
It's upsetting that my mind
would do this to me.
I shouldn't be left alone up there.
Although a faded memory now,
it will always be a reminder
to never take it for granted or abuse it.
I'm still here, a veteran now.

Helping others is priceless.
Giving back to the world
puts out positive energy.
It also shows you how others
view certain aspects in life.
We all die in the end.
So for me when I have something
someone really needs I help them.
I can do without.
When people say they feel fulfilled,
for me I feel empty.
Not in a negative way.
I'm so used to my body being in constant
chaos that in times like these I feel
nothing.
It's nice.

Throughout life people come and go.
Some can do you wrong.
Those that experience wrong doing, but still must have the perpetrators in their world should look past the negativity for their own peace of mind.
So everytime you see them in future they will know they done you wrong, but you rose above the usual reaction one would expect from betrayal.
Kill them with kindness.
Be a real one.

A shadow of yourself,
trying to navigate through the darkness.
Forever lost.
Destroyed by unspeakable trauma.
Social connections faded.
How can you come back from it?
Time is frozen.
Your scars thicken.
It will never leave you.
Becoming numb is the outcome.
The suffering in my thoughts
for myself and others alike is heavy.
Others go through life
forgetting about them.
In my world,
they will always have a shoulder.
My arms forever wide apart.
The broken will always be welcome.

"I'm trying to be good".
Words that many have said and still say.
Aiming for temporary goals.
Maybe they see others going through life looking or feeling fantastic.
So they feel the need to try and be good.
If it isn't your lifestyle then stop.
Try being you and only you.
Try understanding who you really are and what your purpose is in this life.
Beats being stuck in a never ending loop of trying, trying and yes one more time, trying.
Master who you really are.
No one is perfect.
Just be you.

I had the most fascinating dream
of my entire life.
I knew all of creation and destruction.
I watched a mountain
explode and destroy everything.
I knew how everything was created.
I questioned it.
Became the question,
and then, became the answer.
I woke up with a tear in my left eye
trying to explain it to my wife, but
couldn't.
It's so hard to explain.

I'm feeling the struggle again.
We are all the same.
Feels impossible to break the stigma.
Death continuously lurking again.
The pain is slowly breaking me.
I'm beginning to lose my cool.
I just want to sleep forever.
Everytime I open my eyes
I am reminded that I am still here
dealing with this mentality, all over again.
The nightmare has returned.
I'm stuck in this maze.
Digging the hole deeper and deeper
trying to get by.
Forever lost.
I am cursed.

Are you an observer?
Do you listen to peoples bullshit?
There's alot of it out there.
Everything is so serious.
I'd rather vanish.
I'm cursed, and that curse is feeding off the ones who lovingly surround me.
Homicidal thoughts toward my own body.
I'll never get the peace I need until I'm dead.
Dealing with this all over again.
Creating ranks amongst my demons.
I see the crooked smiles.
My vessel is the veteran.
Broken and scarred.
My heart is cold.
I want to feel alive, but
my heart is cold.

The new year is upon us.
Never was one for the whole
"new year, new me".
I'm giving everything up.
Everything I go through
has me going insane.
My figure eight world
will slowly navigate a new route.
I want to float over my past
releasing my negative energy.
Entrust in yourself.
Society is designed to keep
the struggling, struggling.
This is a journey you must conquer
alone.
Toe to toe with the creatures that latch
onto you, one by one they will roll away.
The poison will be drained.

Dueling with my mind,
makes the time go by.
One day I'm going to wake up
and look in the mirror and
see an old timer with no time.
My night terrors are day terrors.
They consume me.
Cut connections to rewire.
There's a thin line between life and death.
Living day to day.
Addictions churning away.
They feed off my weaknesses.
Spectating my own insanity.
It will never stop,
but I won't accept defeat.
I wish I could cut myself deep enough
and
pull a better version of me out.
I handle myself.

Suffering sells.
Peace does not.
Once you find a way to escape the mind,
fill the hole you dug.
Wipe away the poison.
Look to your left, look to your right.
Walk out of that maze.
The one you couldn't escape.
Once a slave.
Back lashed with invisible scars.
A free man.

Ambition is the competition.
No one gets it.
So take your back up off against that wall. Move it!
Taking nothing for granted.
Tongue tied for so long.
Your blood is flowing.
Burn the leeches.
No more feeding.
You are your own master.
Was designed, now resigned.
Prisoner no more.
Create your own symphony.
Repeat it in your head.
Heart beat, heart beat.
Lead and move to its kick-snare.
Entire life's vibrations universally paired.

All the universe asks of you is an offering. An offering of your strongest vibrations.
Searching for that aligned feeling, loosening up that grip on fake reality.
This worlds movie will always continue.
Foggy isn't it.
Howling and growling, respect your haul.
Gradually unloading.
Warm breath so clear.
Loading of a new haul.
Balance radiating.
Signs of miracles past the hellfire.
Latches broke.
On the front foot.
Don't hit the ground.
Though scarred, paralysed footprints go on and on.
Gravitational force, never looking back, pulls us through the darkness wondering, who is there.

Life is an impulse.
Lost in a war.
Thug tears.
Making enemies.
Impulses counteract.
Kindness taken for weakness.
Making chess moves.
He who poses as a fool is not a fool.
Seperate understanding.
Analysing who's who.
Bearing scars of defeat.
Closed roads become distant memories.

Eyes are drowsy.
Lungs filling rapidly.
Wreckless breathing.
Mind throttling.
Forgive and forget.
Combat boots worn out.
An act is a commitment.
It radiates.
Emotions, but not for others.
Self acceptance is the purpose.
I'm feeling that.

Four months have passed.
I start writing again.
Stuck in an endless loop of ups and downs.
An addict to rock bottoms.
It's said that you need to hit rock bottom before you can regain control of your life.
I reject most help, trying to regain alone.
Trauma faced as a child becomes the face.
Sounds of chains clinking.
An echoing scream within.
The eyes tell an invisible story.
Attempts at painting a picture of the mind kills within.
Your attentions drawn,
I runaway.

You can tell levels of intelligence by the mannerisms and reactions of another.
A velvet fog surrounds many.
I talk to myself,
because I am my own consultant.
Progressive thinking from a young old man.
Start from scratch.
Over and over again, if you need too.
A heavy heart needs to rebuild.
Struggling can damage your pride.
Broke like a promise.
You feel every test.
Calculate problems.
An endless mind is capable of anything.
Drain the negative energy from your body.
Keep your aura positive at all costs.
Zero regrets.

I want to reiterate,
"If I can't get you when you're awake,
I'll get you in your dreams".
Feeling solid lately.
Although,
when your body has been programmed
from a young age to only know anxiety
you are reminded of this once again.
Now awake,
My wife softly caresses my back, and
I asked her, "can you feel that"?
She replies, "feel what"?
To which I reply, "exactly".
Regardless of any details in the dream
and as vivid as it was,
I'm calm.
Now, I analyse my train of thought
seeking to understand this.
It's acceptance, I already know,
but if you find yourself experiencing this,
learn to understand your mind.

Conquer your paranoia.
We can all get paranoid at some point, but unfortunately some can be tortured by it.
When you are dealing with a paranoid episode, which can be something really happening to you or that you have slowly created believing to be true then, try exploring yourself in every aspect.
Tell yourself repeatedly that you don't care.
Learn to train your mind to focus on what's really important, that being, the real you!
Don't let your mind get sucked down a rabbit hole of meaningless nothingness.
Paranoia is a waste of time.
Don't let yourself be stuck in the middle.
Pull yourself out and focus on your entirety.
Accept who you are as a human being.
Love, and never ever doubt yourself.
Stay in control of your journey.

You can choose any route.
Make sure it's always a positive one.

Liars.
When you know someone is lying, they know you know, but they hold onto it for a bit, then admit their wrong doing certainly breaks trust.
The worst type of lies are actually small and quite frankly meaningless ones.
If a person chooses to lie over the smallest of things it can make you question much deeper assumptions you've made in the past, but in these situations they never backed down.
Now this can fall under paranoia for the most part, but when you can read peoples body language, you know.
To reiterate on paranoia don't let yourself be stuck in the middle.
Learn to seperate yourself from such actions of another and continue on with your own journey.
Moving on is accepting, not forgetting.

I didn't know the difference between reality and imagination.
A teddy bear became a lifeless baby that I held slowly bringing back to life, but it kept dying, so to keep it alive I continuously rubbed it's head to stay warm.
Chased through my house by nonexistent vessels as they try to stab me.
Arguments with people who weren't there trying to reason with them to leave my home.
Vivid, now a dense ghostly fog.
I'm scarred from the trauma.

You can't control your surroundings,
but you can try and control how you feel.
With precise decision making,
work on rules, rules to live by.
Benefit from the structure set by them.
Never neglect your strengths.
Feelings can crumble you in an instant.
Some of us are moulded deep to our core
by the feelings we didn't know how to
cope with, which, with no understanding
of how to cope with coping,
we are forever in our feelings.
Learn a way to shut your feelings off.
A remedy that can free up time
that usually leaves you lost in your mind.
Integrity.

What is the meaning of life?

To live.

"I think the saddest people always try their hardest to make people happy. Because they know what it feels like to feel absolutely worthless and they don't want anybody else to feel like that."

Robin Williams
1951-2014
RIP

A journey in mental health literature.
There's no way to end this book because the mental health saga will most likely continue until my time is up.
I have written these words over many years trying to word my mind appropriately.
I just hope that you have found some peace in them.
This is a quest towards a goal and that goal is to reach as many minds as possible, cleansing with hopefulness in reprogramming thought patterns.

Until next time.

Mental Health Song

Yo, listen up, I got a story to share,
About mental health,
a topic about which we should all be aware,
It's time to break the stigma,
let's make it clear,
That our minds matter,
it's time to persevere.
Sometimes we're struggling,
feeling lost and alone,
Battling demons inside,
trying to find our own zone,
But we gotta reach out,
let our voices be known,
Together we're stronger,
we can build a new throne.

(Chorus)
Mental health, it's time to rise,
Break the chains, reach for the skies,
Let's fight the darkness, one step at a time,
We're in this together, your hand in mine.

(Verse 2)
Depression, anxiety,
they try to bring us down,
But we won't let them define us,
we'll turn it around,
With therapy and self-care,
we'll heal profound,
Discovering our worth,
our inner strength we've found.
Don't be afraid to seek help,
you're not alone,
Talking to a friend,
or a professional on the phone,

There's no shame in needing
support to condone,
It's a sign of strength,
a testament to how you've grown.

(Chorus)
Mental health, it's time to rise,
Break the chains, reach for the skies,
Let's fight the darkness, one step at a time,
We're in this together, your hand in mine.

(Verse 3)
In this fast-paced world,
we're all under stress,
But let's prioritize self-care,
no more second guess,
Take time for mindfulness,
to relieve the mess,
A peaceful mind and soul,
that's true progress.

Spread love and kindness,
it's a healing embrace,
Support each other, create a safe space,
Break the silence, let's erase the disgrace,
Together we can make a difference, embrace mental health's grace.

(Chorus)
Mental health, it's time to rise,
Break the chains, reach for the skies,
Let's fight the darkness, one step at a time,
We're in this together, your hand in mine.

Printed by Amazon Italia Logistica S.r.l.
Torrazza Piemonte (TO), Italy